All Scripture references taken from the KJV of the Holy Bible, unless otherwise indicated.

Without Form: *Finish the Work*

by Dr. Marlene Miles

Freshwater Press 2024

freshwaterpress9@gmail.com

ISBN: 978-1-963164-42-8

Paperback Version

Copyright 2024, Dr. Marlene Miles

All rights reserved. No part of this book may be reproduced, distributed, or transmitted by any means or in any form including photocopying, recording or other electronic or mechanical methods without prior written permission of the publisher except in the case of brief publications or critical reviews.

Table of Contents

Void & Without Form 5
The Devil Got In It 9
Blood Pollution 19
Be Made Whole 24
Prayer to Renounce Witchcraft 31
Loss of Humanity 33
The Voids... 51
Sin Keeps You Formless 54
Jesus Finished the *Work* 61
Age of Accountability 63
Slimed 65
Entropy: War in Heaven 72
Not Falling Apart... 75
Dismantled... 82
Don't Come Down off the Wall 86
You Are A Prophet 89
Where Are Your Children?...................................... 95
It's So Easy.. 98
Where Is God's Son? 101
Psalm 18:37-50 106
Dear Reader 109
Other books by this author 110

Without Form

Finish the Work

The earth is defiled by its people; they have disobeyed the laws, violated the statutes and broken the everlasting covenant.

Therefore a curse consumes the earth; its people must bear their guilt. Therefore earth's inhabitants are burned up, and very few are left   (Isaiah 24: 5-6 NIV)

Void & Without Form

> In the beginning God created the heaven and the earth. And the earth was without form, and void; and darkness was upon the face of the deep.
> (Genesis 1:1-2)

And the Earth was void and without form. Darkness was over the face of the Deep. Everything God created was not only good, but everything also has personality. *The Deep* has a face. Gates have ears. Mountains can hear; they can move from place to place when spoken to, if a man has faith. Trees die when cursed; they can hear, and so on. All of creation is alive because God does not make dead things. Living things grow, listen, hear, do; they exist. They live and have *being*. The fact that God spoke to the heavens and the Earth, and they obeyed showed that they were not inanimate; they were alive, and obedient.

God had created the Heaven *and* the Earth. Why was there no darkness over the face of Heaven, but there was darkness over the face of the Earth? What happened to the *form* that God created the Earth to have?

A war had broken out in Heaven and Lucifer had been kicked out; he had fallen from Heaven like lightning and where had he fallen to? Earth.

God is Light; the devil is not. The devil's kingdom is one of darkness. Satan had landed on Earth, then **Earth began to take on Satan's nature**; darkness was over the face of the deep, and the Earth was void and without form. That is the devil's nature: dark, void, and formless.

If something is without form, it means it is not solid. Liquids are not solid, neither are gases and spirits. Nonsolid things are changeable, that's good if something is malleable, but if it is mutable, that's bad because that thing can be too easily changed by winds of doctrine. Without form, man is unstable.

We are born as babies in every sense here, and we must grow, develop, and *become*.

We must grow physically. We must grow emotionally, and intellectually, and we must develop spiritually. We must be watered. We need Living Water to live and to thrive. The Lord is my shepherd. He leads me beside the still waters, and those are waters of peace.

In Genesis, at the watering hole, Jacob's cattle reproduced after what they saw and that's what they *became. W*hat the cows were looking *at, that's what* they produced; they produce after *that kind.* We must *become* as well. We are mandated to be fruitful and multiply, and ultimately, we will reproduce after our kind. If *our kind* is whole and possesses our peace, that is what we will produce and reproduce. If we are in the form, the image, and the likeness of God, we will produce after God's kind, both in body and in spirit.

The image and likeness of God is a definite image. We have a physical body so we can do that.

The devil on the other hand is a *spirit*, so unless he takes over a body, he has no body for this Earth. He is without a clear or definite shape or structure which is why he is wily, subtle, and has been successful in masquerades, disguises, turning himself into an angel of light, and making people think that he doesn't exist as he does his evil. He can be amorphous, which is how he can be without form, therefore whatever worships or follows him takes on that indefinite, formless, shape-shifting nature.

We are born on Earth into a physical body. We are born spiritually weak, but if we stay that way, we are at risk for being stolen from, killed, destroyed, even sacrificed, like lambs going to slaughter. As with cattle, we must grow up, and not be veal.

The Devil Got In It

The Earth that God made and had said**, It is good**, had become void and without form. Just by the fact that God made Earth, we know that it was perfect and excellent; God does not make half-way, sort-of, or trash.

At this point, darkness was over the face of the Deep because the devil had gotten into it.

God also had made man, and had again said**, "It is good**." But the devil got into man also, and man began to take on the nature of the devil.

Soon after, others began to be born into that sin nature, and shaped in iniquity, because man began to multiply *after his kind*. This kind, though, was the *kind* that man had *become,* **not** the kind- -- the perfect man prototype that God had created.

God's original creation, Adam and the *other* Adam who the male Adam named Eve were perfect, flawless both spiritually and physically--, in every way. When God told them to be fruitful and multiply, God was expecting them to make more of themselves, like themselves, **before** they sinned. (Genesis 1:28).

God gave man charge to make the Earth what He intended it to be, that is the perfect man over Earth that needed work. Earth had been created by God and it was good; I know this because God said it. But now, darkness was over the face of the Deep. Somehow Earth had been abased. --Oh, the devil got in it when he fell from Heaven, like lightning.

God's creation, man, sinned and then devolved quickly into an imperfect man, staring at an Earth that was void and without form. Somehow man had become like what he was looking at; an Earth that was void and without *form*. As the Earth had begun to take on the nature of Satan, when man sinned, so did man take on that nature.

All this, after sin and after he had begun to reproduce and multiply after his kind--, his new kind which was not improved; it was downgraded devil-style.

Sometimes we can't see who we are until we see what we have made. Sometimes what we have made is just standing there, staring back at us. Somehow that something can be void, and *without form*--, at least not in the form that we thought it should have been in. Yet, it is after our *kind*. Quite sobering, isn't it?

Authorized to become a son of God, man is set in dominion and that is a position of authority and power. But man traded that unknowingly when he sinned. From there man took on a sin-nature.

When we minister to others, or are being ministered to, we are working to bring a man out of formlessness and out of darkness, or to come out of it ourselves. Sometimes we fall into darkness, sometimes we are tricked into it, or dragged into it. But to live and prosper, we must come out of the void, out of being *without* FORM--, that form being the form of God, the image and likeness of God. Our goal is to bring ourselves, and others into the marvelous Light of Jesus Christ, take on His image and **His** nature.

But man kept sinning because sin is anointed to beget more sin.

> Whoever makes a practice of sinning is of the devil, for the devil has been sinning from the beginning. The reason the Son of God appeared was to destroy the works of the devil.
> (1 John 3:8 ESV)

Let us make man in our own image, God said. That is, the *FORM*, the image of God. We are not God, but Jesus, the firstborn of many brethren, and our Spiritual Supermodel thought it not robbery to be equal with God.

> Who, being in the form of God, thought it not robbery to be equal with God:
>
> But made himself of no reputation, and took upon him the form of a servant, and was made in the likeness of men: (Philippians 2:6-7)

The devil cannot block God from making anything and least of all block God from making something in His own image and likeness. But the devil works to block **man**, stop **man**, unravel **man**, empty, waste, destroy, devour, and swallow up the efforts of man. Most of the efforts of man are the man changing from what he was when he got here on Earth, to what he should be. That includes growing, developing, and progressing. In that process we change from one form to another. The goal is to change from being full of voids to reaching completion.

> The LORD will perfect *that which* concerneth me: thy mercy, O LORD, *endureth* for ever: forsake not the works of thine own hands. (Psalm 138:8)

To perfect a matter, a person or a thing in this sense means to complete it, to carry it through to the end. Jesus was the Perfect Man meaning He was complete, and He was not defective; He had no faults in Him and He was the express image and likeness of God, in a man. That includes being complete in moral excellence, as well.

> Be ye therefore *perfect* even as your Father who is in heaven is *perfect.* (Matthew 5:48)

Man must *become* who he is supposed to be in God before he can fully and properly do the assignment, the work that he was put here to do. Except God gives us Grace and by His own patience He allows us on-the-job training, else, how long would we wait to start anything related to purpose or destiny? No human is perfect; if you are waiting for perfection to begin anything, including ministry, you will wait idle and unfulfilled.

A hundred or so years on Earth is a short time to learn what we may need to know from a God who has lived from everlasting to everlasting, from eternity and to infinity. In the natural, it takes many people 20 or more years to master the job that they went to school for; this is why most professions call what they do, *practice*.

Spiritual things are considered harder, as many lessons are invisible, so you have to use your spirit man to learn them. What your flesh learns, versus what your soul learns, versus what your spirit learns, and which one will you lean on when you need support in a matter tells God, you, and others who you are.

My destiny is integral to my **form**; my form is integral to my destiny. My purpose is to achieve my FORM, **and** reach spiritual perfection, in Christ.

We are so worried about our physical form, while God is looking at our spirit man. The physical form will rot; it rots from day to day unless God preserves you. We spend so much time on our bodies to make it reach some perfect form. It is important for us to do and complete our work, but our bodies are not the only thing that must achieve *form*. Our physical body is the measure of health in the natural, unless the mind goes haywire. Spiritual interferences are too often the last thing to be noticed by most people, but all four of those aspects of our being are important.

Do you want a fantastic body or a well-developed spirit man? Both? Which do you want first? Which do you want the most? And in between that, have you given any thought to the development of your soul?

God preserves us spiritually; we strengthen our spirit man which is what sustains us in times of trouble and so that we are preserved physically. The spirit man impacts our soul and also sustains the physical man. Our souls need to achieve their perfected **form**, going from immature to prospered.

Without form is the nature of the devil; he makes things to become after his kind, even if that means dismantling even what is good, if he can gain access to it. The devil uses amorphousness, ambivalence, as a tactic against man and for his attacks. He comes in many forms, while **Jesus Christ is the same yesterday**, today, and forever. Jesus changes not.

The devil is a chameleon.

We change but it should be a progression, a progressive change, not demonic or backward changes.

Some humans cop out and think it's easier to be vague and not fully into anyone or anything. In the natural some call that non-committal. That is, we don't commit to anything or any particular way, we don't settle on being what we actually are or should be. Those people can be called flaky, flighty, or mercurial, for example.

This is seen in men who refuse to marry; they don't commit to any woman. Suspect the nature of Satan at work in that man whether he realizes it or not.

> Beloved I wish above all things that you would prosper and be in health, even as your soul prospers. (3 John 2)

I recently saw a movie where a man with no business savvy was set up in business and as soon as he saw revenue coming in, he began to live large off of it. He ate the first morning's revenue for lunch. Because the people in the restaurant recognized him as a fool, they flattered him, so then he bought lunch for everyone in the restaurant.

Each day he became more and more extravagant because he was stealing all the income from a business where he paid nothing toward the expenses of that enterprise. This man had no soul prosperity, and it was to the demise of the business, others, and ultimately himself. Achieving soul prosperity is part of attaining Godly form.

When we do not invest spiritually in the things of God, He will not let us have what we think we should have sometimes. Mainly because God knows what we would do or how it may ruin us if we receive great blessings before our souls are prospered. We must learn first, so we don't abuse blessings, gifts, and "profits."

What does it profit a man to gain the whole world, but lose his soul? What does it gain a man who was made in the image and likeness of God, but then takes on the nature of the devil because it's fun, or easy, or makes him feel good or important? There is no spiritual investment in God when a man does that, and he is putting his own soul up for collateral to get *things and stuff* from Satan.

Is there a man who has paid the devil back for even any small thing the evil one did for that man? It is virtually impossible, so the devil takes that soul.

A soulless man is void and *without form.* What can that man reproduce in his mandate to be fruitful and multiply, after his kind?

Blood Pollution

> And when I passed by thee, and saw thee polluted in thine own blood, I said unto thee *when thou wast* in thy blood, Live; yea, I said unto thee *when thou wast* in thy blood, Live.
> Ezekiel 16:6

Polluted blood in the natural, leads to diseases, such as leukemia, blood cancers, or sepsis. The verse above is about **spiritually polluted blood**. Does God take us out of our polluted blood? In a sense, when He adopts us and puts us into His family. He puts us into a new family. New family--, new blood.

Does He take the polluted blood out of us? In the Old Testament He *covered*. Now that we are under the Better Blood, we ask God to transfuse us and put us into His family and out of the sinful family that we may have been born into. No disrespect to mom and dad, but we have no idea of what pollutants our ancestors may have caused to be in the blood of our bloodline. If they didn't cause it, we don't know if they tried to block it from happening, and why haven't they prayed it out of our bloodline yet?

Sin pollutes blood.

The blood that God intended for us to have, He made and put in Adam and Eve. That blood was to multiply in their fruitfulness. Adam and Eve were evicted from the Garden and may have been thinking, *Hey, we're still alive, so I guess we did okay after all. We'll just downsize until we can save up and move back into the Garden, or a nicer place than what we have right now.*

But they weren't still alive.

Sin makes a man take in tainted, poison waters. Sin makes a man take on the nature of the devil. Sin pollutes the blood of a man. Sin kills.

Adam and Eve sinned, then the next thing you know they reproduce *after their kind* and here comes a killer--, Cain. But do they even recognize that their own child is *after their kind* and their *kind* has changed from perfect, as they used to be, to *this*? They weren't still alive, they had committed suicide; they were killers. **They had killed themselves by sinning,** therefore they could produce a killer, after their *kind*.

Why is the blood important? Because it's like the starter of sour dough or kombucha, it carries forward, and it gets into **every** subsequent generation. What is in the blood is what we will make; that is the *kind* that we will produce. Well, one of our offspring could go rogue on their own. (And, that can happen, too.) But usually what is in us is what we make. There it is--, staring right at us.

Blood is spiritual although we can see it in the natural. The blood goes forward and backward all through time, unlike flesh. Flesh rots: the blood lives forever.

Where in the Bible did anyone *kill* blood? Or, destroy blood? Hide blood? Nowhere. It is impossible. Even using the strongest chemicals that we have available to us today, there is always a trace of blood that can be found on surfaces and clothing. Even if man can't see it any more, it is still there. God can see it and hear it; if it were not so, then Abel's blood would have fully deteriorated by now, but it is still crying out from the ground. We know this because the Law of Sin and Death is still at work.

There is a young woman who found out that her mother was into witchcraft, at what level or what kind, she doesn't really know. But she said when she found out she started going to church herself, more and more. Of course, being a good Catholic, she doesn't know that it takes more than that because if her mother is a witch, or if her father were a warlock, she is automatically born a witch. It is in the blood.

This daughter loves, loves, loves cats and has no idea that this is an emotional expression flowing from what is in her blood. (No, I am not saying that cat lovers or cat owners are witches.) She also has other pets that are historically *witchy*. She is oblivious to all of this due to a lack of knowledge.

The spirit lives on, the soul lives on, the blood lives on. The soul identifies you as one of God's by you being *of* Adam, *of* Eve, *of* Abraham, *of* Isaac, et cetera, and adopted into the lineage of Jesus Christ. By the blood.

The ways we get into a family are by adoption, or being born into it--, related by birth, or by marriage and covenant. When you have sex with a person, you are now related to them; they are your spouse. You already have a spouse? Then you're a polygamist.

When the body is exsanguinated, the individual will die. We need air, water, food and **blood** to live. We need unpolluted blood to live a physically healthy and spiritually healthy life.

Blood can be abused, and I go into that in my book, **When You See Blood.** We need the devil out of our lives and out of our blood because it determines what we will produce, either as the works of our hands or the fruit of our loins.

Be Made Whole

God begat Jesus; but God doesn't just want one Son, God wants many sons.

One who becomes a son of God must have a whole soul. Whole means complete, but it also means finished and perfected. Until a baby grows it is vulnerable. Until a soul prospers it is easily influenced or tampered with. Until a man fully *forms*, he may be subject to suggestions, influences, pressure--- even evil pressure, and he may be mutable. Changing by winds of doctrine will toss a man about and it may cause him to take on the nature of that which is tossing him. In a storm at sea, even a large ship is tossed. The winds do the tossing, in the natural, and also winds of doctrine.

Demons that invade a man's soul will toss it every which way.

One cannot become a whole soul until he expels strangers (strange *gods* from his soul); that is deliverance. You can maintain your deliverance by resistance, and *becoming,* living a Godly lifestyle, and finishing the work that you were sent to Earth to do.

If you are a serious student, you cannot finish your coursework and earn your degree, that is, matriculate until you get those party loving, frat boy roommates out of your dorm room so you can focus and study.

We are responsible for making our souls prosper. We should prosper more each day reaching toward the image of God. We cannot accidentally become like God, there are too many interferences, choices, tricks, and traps to keep us from that. Just as there are too many frat boys in the dorm, spiritually, there are too many idol *gods* in the world, interfering, testing, tempting, trying us and trying to force their nature on us.

Therefore hath the curse **devour**ed the earth, and they that dwell therein are desolate: therefore the inhabitants of the earth are burned, and few men left. (Isaiah 24:6)

Will you be made whole? Jesus healed the multitude. Why would a multitude of people need to be healed? Why were so many sick? Was there a pandemic going on then? Was there a plague? No, there was widespread sin, so there was sin sickness. Because of that people were generally sick and they were unhealed and unwhole, unprospered, and unformed. They were not fully formed, even though they may have been grown up, they were not in the image and likeness of God.

Every disease, disorder or sickness is an attack against man reaching the image and likeness of God. God is never sick or ill. Jesus was not sick.

Let's say a man is growing more into the image of God every day. But, every time he is sick or gets sick, physically, spiritually, mentally, or emotionally, that will either stop his growth, and/or break down or dismantle the progress he has already made.

Now, I'm not saying that God can't use sickness to build a man, change a man, make him more compassionate, and empathetic, because God can. But we don't seek after sickness; being ill is not holy and diseases are **not** "put on us by God." And, since disease and illness are under the Curse of the Law, we should never embrace an illness or give it the title, *my* or *mine.*

Sin afflicts the soul of man. When the soul is afflicted, it affects the physical body. The ***notification*** that we are sin sick and have soul affliction is disease or disorder in the body.

- Lord, I repent of sinning against You. Lord, have Mercy on me, a sinner. Forgive me of my sins, the sins of my parents and my ancestors, take away all iniquity from my bloodline, in the Name of Jesus.
- Lord, if I am none of Yours, come into my heart today and make me one of Yours, in the Name of Jesus.

Sicknesses and diseases belong to the devil; it is an evil load that he imposes on man and has been successful at making a man carry that illness--, sometimes unto death.

- Powers in my soul waiting in line to manifest sickness in my body, I forbid your manifestation, by the power in the Blood of Jesus.

- Powers in my soul sponsoring affliction, disease, or sickness, get out! Get out! By Fire and by Force get out, die out of my soul, in the Name of Jesus.

Demons in our soul cause us to take on their nature. Their nature is SIN. In the New Testament it says that Jesus went about healing all that were sick, and He cast out many devils. *The devil you say?* No, the devil is what the Bible says. As soon as the demons were cast out people were healed that self-same hour. People were even raised from the dead.

Jesus took on the sins of the world. Well, He gave up the Ghost but all that sin--, the sins of **all mankind** would kill a person anyway. Think about that, the sin of all mankind was all that were living at that time; not just those around the Cross for the spectacle of it, but all the sin of the whole world at that time. And, now Time must be considered again because it is the sin of all those living then to the time when Jesus returns.

Some of the sin we commit that we think is just a little sin, is still sin and meant to KILL. So,

the sin of the world would definitely kill a man. But Jesus was not just man, He was also all God, therefore by knowing that He gave up the Ghost meant that what would kill the average person, Jesus wouldn't have died from, but He didn't. Jesus could have saved Himself, but He didn't; He saved us.

JESUS CARRIED *OUR* EVIL LOAD TO THE CROSS AT CALVARY.

After sin, first the person becomes spiritually dead, then its lights out from there. The lights could go out slowly and barely noticeably to the person, or it could be all at once. If you are spiritually dead that means the devil is in charge of you, except for the Mercy of God.

By carrying all that sin, Jesus was relegated outside of the Gates of Heaven for the time that he was in Sheol or Hell. We know that the way God was bragging on Job by asking, **Have you considered my servant Job?** And by the way Satan was gloating over what evil he had done to Job, what was happening with Jesus had to be the *most* extreme, since the devil knew who

Jesus was even though so many in Jerusalem had missed their visitation.

It's still the same today--, the devil knows who you are and who you are supposed to become, even if you don't. If you are convinced that the form you were born with is your real form, you are mistaken. And that's just what he wants, it's why he changed God's form, or messes with your mind to keep you from seeing your real form and fights you from attaining to your Godly form even if you do figure it out and try to reach it.

Lights out puts the sin sick soul in darkness. Put any plant in the dark and see if it will live. We are trees of righteousness, the planting of the Lord. We must have light to move, breathe, have being, to see and to grow. In Genesis 1:3 God said let there be Light. That tells us there that darkness had encroached into the Earth, so God had to call for light.

Jesus gave up the Ghost because of the Prophecy that not a bone on Him would be broken. Therefore, Jesus gave up the Ghost so that His legs would not be broken to hasten death. After hanging on the Cross for some hours, if the victim is not dead by sunset (or a certain time), his legs would be broken to facilitate the asphyxiation. Roman soldiers were cruel and did as they were told. Without guns, that would be the same as busting a cap in the knees of the person already nailed to a Cross.

Look at all that Jesus went through to give you the opportunity to be restored to right form and fullness in the Lord. Shall you not access that?

Prayer to Renounce Witchcraft

Father, I come to You in the Name of Jesus Christ. I confess Lord that I have participated in _____, which means that I came into agreement with the evil works of darkness. I acknowledge this is sin before You and I repent and renounce all involvement in the wicked works of darkness. I ask You to forgive me and wash me clean in the Blood of Jesus Christ.

I choose this day Lord, to follow You and I forsake all attachments and agreements with the unfruitful works of darkness.

Prayer for Deliverance

I now bind and cast out every demonic spirit in my soul given entrance through these occult sins. I am not in agreement with you, and I cast you out now! Leave this house and go where Jesus Christ of Nazareth tells you to go now!

I declare I am FREE because whom the Son sets free is FREE INDEED! Thank You, Jesus, for Your great love and mercy. Thank You for loving me and setting me free to serve you all the days of my life. I choose to go all in with You 100%, in the name of Jesus. Amen.

Both prayers above taken from https://fromtheheartogod.wordpress.com/effective-prayers/prayers-of-repentance/repentance-prayers-for-occult-activities-witchcraft-satanism/

Loss of Humanity

You lost part of your humanity, by sinning, by works of the flesh. This sinning includes witchcraft because it makes you hard hearted. One has to be cold hearted to practice the craft; it is part of the initiation, whether folks believe that or not. Sin chips away at your humanity. So, if the devil can't get you all at once, he'll be happy taking your humanity bit by bit, chip by chip.

If you want to stay jealous, hurt, or in unforgiveness or you want to stay in bitterness, this allows the devil entrance to take pieces of you away until you are diminished, or you're all the way used up, all the way gone.

You've heard people say about others, "*I don't think he's all there*". Well, maybe he's not. Maybe parts of his humanity have been lost or locked away and he could still be just walking around looking alive, appearing to be alive, but he's spiritually dead, like a soulless zombie. Adam and Eve looked like they were still alive when they were spiritually dead. They were even having children, **while spiritually dead.** Again, that is how they produced Cain.

Don't you be the person who has become evil and hateful or cold and uncaring because of losing the warm and compassionate part of your soul. You may not even know that it is gone or has been locked away. *Lights out* could be on a dimmer switch for you, going out very slowly, almost imperceptibly, rather than the entire light bulb just blowing all at once.

If you've closed yourself off from the Spirit of God there's no way to get those lost parts of your humanity back, except by God and the Spirit of Deliverance. **HE RESTORES MY SOUL. That's what that means.**

Any time you close any part of your humanity off from God, you've created a void--, meaning that the Spirit of God is not in that place in your soul This also means that you've allowed the devil in to those places not occupied by the Holy Spirit.

Once in, the devil takes, perverts, or ruins whatever he can steal, kill, destroy, or devour, step by step. If not all at once, then part by part, piece by piece. Most of the time it is so subtle that you don't even realize that anything is happening. It's like putting together a 2000-piece jigsaw puzzle and not realizing that three or four pieces are missing until the very end. If you don't have all the pieces of a jigsaw puzzle it will never achieve its right *form* or image. You could have been so relaxed putting that puzzle together until you got to the end and were shocked that you couldn't finish the work.

Don't let that be your life. Don't be so busy moving the pieces of your life around until you find out at the end that you cannot achieve the image and the likeness of the One who sent you because vital pieces are missing. Don't wait too late to find that those pieces have been stolen or destroyed, stopping you from finishing your work.

The Word says to possess your soul, your whole soul, not just some of it or most of it. That means that all of your soul should be under subjection of your spirit man, which should be under auspices of the Holy Spirit of God. That is the correct form to aspire to, with no voids.

Like those thousand little pores in an English muffin, demons will come to situate themselves in any and every void in your soul. Their goal is to replace the Holy Spirit. Where the Spirit of God would be imparting the nature of God to us, demonic *spirits*, even those mimicking the Holy Spirit will begin to impart their sin nature to their host/victim. Remember, they came from Heaven with Lucifer when he fell, and they are 100% rebellious. No one who wants to be **like** God *leaves* God.

The serpent in the Garden was described as subtle. Insidious insertion of even one demonic *spirit* is the beginning of the erosion of the God-nature of even an innocent soul.

Has the goodness of your soul been eroded? Was it so subtle that you didn't even notice?

You may have participated, unknowingly. Locking off parts of your humanity is by your agreement and your own decision, such as when you refuse to forgive, continue to sin, or, if you choose to hate another or another people group, for example. Racism is done by souls that are in captivity. So is ageism, sexism – any *ism*, any hatred toward a person, people, or people group is because of a **loss of humanity**, empathy, compassion in the racist, and that is because that soul is captive by some *spirit* or *spirits* that are not the Holy Spirit.

When people lose their humanity, they may become robotic, zombie-like, Stepford spouse-like; they are going through the motions, just going through life, doing what everyone else is doing--, what *people* are doing, and not what God is doing. Your soul is the very thing that makes you totally unique goes missing or when it's damaged, when it's foreshortened, it's as though you lose your identity. A person could become apathetic, sad, depressed. A person could be the happiest frat boy on campus and never know that his soul has been compromised, captive--, at least, *not at first*.

The Word of God says we are to possess our souls in sanctification and honor. We are to prosper our souls.

> Beloved, I wish above all things you would prosper and be in health even as your soul prospers. (3 John 2)

God would not have told us to *possess* our souls unless there was going to be an issue, a challenge, or some type of attack regarding possessing our own souls. When you send your kid off to school or college and you give them certain valuable possessions, do you not tell them to be sure to come back home with that item or items? Of course, you do. God is like that, too; that's why He said: **Possess ye your souls**.

Whatever you used to sin with, that's what and where the devil can access to attack you and perhaps even destroy that thing, especially; but all of your being is at risk. Whether personal sin, ancestral and generational sin, not even full-blown evil dedication, sin has been rampant and organized in a bloodline for so many generations that the devil just has full access to that whole family.

But whatever body part you sinned with, or you used to sin with, you grant the devil access to that part of your body, that part of your soul, that part of your spirit, and your life.

So, you wake up from some crazy dream one morning, be it a one-time dream, or a repetitive dream, you better find out what that dream means because is that God trying to tell you something? Probably. If not, is the devil trying to attack you? Either way, you need to know the proper interpretation, so you know how to pray. Dreams are not night videos, night mini-series, or telenovelas to give you something to talk about with your friends, so you can say, *I had this crazy dream*.

No, you have got work to do. And in doing that work you are acknowledging that there is a spirit world, and that you know about it and are a part of it. Ultimately, you are acknowledging that you are a spirit, and that is essential knowledge to perfecting your *form*--, completing the work regarding your *form*.

Speak the Word of God against any evil dream and tell the devil what he's going to do and what he's not going to do as it pertains to you, your family, or the people for whom you pray. You speak, you give voice to the Word of God. Resist the devil and he will flee from you.

When you're asleep, you may be in severe warfare. You might have a Word problem, that would be if you're not studying the Word, reading, and getting the Word in you, and building up your spirit man. **That** is a Word problem.

You can't just be floating through life thinking, *Ohh, I'm saved*. This is not a cartoon; this is your real life. And you think you're just going to have a life of leisure, living your best life. Well, spiritually thinking that, hey, since you accepted Jesus, you got baptized, you have anything else to do? Yeah, you do. You have lots more to do because the devil does not respect you.

The devil has a battering ram, trying to break down the doors of your house, the gates of your city, the walls of your life, but many people don't even believe he exists. Your fortified towns, and man-made fortifications may make you think you're secure, but when something devastating happens and you don't believe the devil exists you will either not fight spiritually, or you will lash out against people. A lot of people make that error, blaming those with flesh and blood for their problems and struggles. That is a strict no-no.

The devil doesn't respect you. Even when you have built your manmade walls for protection, it doesn't matter to the devil. Fortresses that are not of God, if they're not in the Spirit, they that watch will watch in vain. Except the Lord build the house, they that labor, labor in vain.

The devil takes advantage of every access point where he can; if you think he doesn't, you're living in a fool's paradise.

Personal sin allows the devil in.

You should have no *voids* in your soul; if you do the Holy Spirit should be invited and allowed there. Else, the devil will get in there.

They say there is an *app* for everything--, there are many apps, but, as usual, God had this first. An ***apse*** is the part of a church where the church's altar is placed.

The devil is trying to get to and capture that part of your heart. The devil is trying to gain entrance into your heart to capture the apse-- or the place of the throne of your heart. Your job is to make sure Jesus is sitting on that Throne and the devil stays out. You do this by your choices 24/7. Yes, even when you are asleep, you are still responsible for what your spirit man is doing.

Stop shutting down parts of your soul. Your intellect, your mind, is a part of your soul. Stop shutting down parts of your humanity. Don't shut down your intellect. Don't say that you will never read a book again because you graduated from high school. Shutting down any part of yourself stagnates your life and stifles the growth and development of your God-intended *form*.

Just because God breathed life into Adam, into man, and he became a living soul, a human being, the devil's going to come for man. Don't make it easy for the devil by shutting down parts of yourself from God. You need to give God access to all of yourself. Love the Lord with all of your being.

> And allow God to love ALL of you. Love the Lord your God with all your heart. And with all your soul, and with all your mind, and with all your strength. (Matthew 12:30)

The devil is after you all day, all night, even in your dreams. You dream in symbols for the most part. The following are examples found in some dreams. Dreams of being lost, trapped, wandering, chased, or attacked by animals, or by people. These are all troubling dreams if you know anything spiritually. If you just think you ate the wrong thing, or watched a violent movie that night, you might let it slide. If you just love animals and think they are cute, you may let an evil animal dream just go by and the devil can do anything he wants to you sooner, or later. Animals should not be in your dreams. Period.

You have to find out what all your dreams mean. Sex in the dream. Marrying people in the dream, marrying people you know, marrying people you don't know, or marrying strangers--, it doesn't matter, it's all bad. Dreaming of dead people is especially foreboding. Some dreams and some people in dreams are masquerades; these are all tricks of the enemy.

Signing documents in a dream--, don't do it. Eating food in a dream, getting injections in a dream are all horrible, disastrous, evil, and demonic dreams. Dreaming of snakes and reptiles--, not good--, you're captive. Cancel those dreams immediately and pray to get out of captivity.

You need to know what your dreams mean from a reputable biblical source or knowledgeable Christian minister. Seek out a reputable person, book, or website. Don't just look your dreams up on psychic or random websites. That will get you in worse trouble. And yes, there are spiritual attacks while you are sleeping and dreaming.

The Kingdom of Heaven is like a man who sowed good seed in his field, but while men slept, his enemy came and sowed tares, (weeds) among the wheat, and went his way. Yes, attacks happen at night.

No matter what the devil or man does there will come a day when we all will have to answer to God if we have resisted Him, His Word, or His Spirit. At the Name of Jesus, every knee will bow. There will be a day of reckoning.

When is it?

I don't know. No one knows. But at the Name of Jesus, every knee should bow of those in heaven, and those on Earth and those under the Earth, And that every tongue should confess that Jesus Christ is Lord to the glory of God the Father.

The devil may be thinking that he can't turn you from saved back to *un*saved, but he is trying to get you bound and heavily yoked and burdened, so you don't do the work that God sent you here to do, and so that you don't live the abundant life that God has for you.

The devil wants to compromise you, if not fully, a bit at a time, a piece at a time. If you have a miserable life, you'll have a horrible testimony that will repel people rather than draw them to Christ. Your witness will be nonexistent, and we are called to be a witness in the Earth by our life, our lifestyle, by our words, by our actions and deeds.

But God will have respect unto you, and He will make covenant with you. He'll give you rain in due season and make you a tree that bears fruit and the harvest you have will minister to you until you sow next year. You won't suffer insufficiency or run out of anything. You will have plenty of bread to eat, and you will dwell in your land safely. There'll be peace in your land.

Nobody's going to make you afraid. Nobody. God will get the evil beasts out of the land, and He will keep war away from your land. And if you chase your enemies, they will run from you. They will be afraid of you.

> I will have respect unto you. And make you fruitful and multiply you and establish my covenant with you. (Leviticus 26:9)

You will have more than enough, and not have to live hand-to-mouth. God says He will Tabernacle among you. Glory to God. God wants to Tabernacle with us. He wants to walk with us and be our God, and we could be His people, the sheep of his pasture.

> For I am the Lord your God, which brought you forth out of the land of Egypt, that you should not be their bondman. And I've broken the bands of your yoke and made you go upright.

These are the things that come from respect, being respected by God and being in covenant with God, whereas the devil has been working against God's creation for centuries. And what he can expect for that is to burn in a lake of fire and brimstone forever, and ever, in eternal damnation, that is not made for man.

Your humanity is part of your *form*. Your prospered, developed soul is critical to becoming all God said you should be because God is Love and the gifts of God work by Love. Without your soul, without a whole soul, you cannot Love.

Pray

I bind up every assignment of witchcraft and sorcerers and diviners against me in the night hours; I command you to stop, cease and desist, let go of God's people.

Lord, open my eyes to see and empower my mind to remember my dreams, in the Name of Jesus.

Holy Ghost Fire, burn up the clouds of confusion and doubt in my mind. Break every mind fog, clear it up by the Blood of Jesus.

I break up every evil altar of every evil worker by the Thunder Hammer of God, in Jesus' Name.

I command all Satanic mirrors to break, in Jesus' Name.

All monitoring *spirits* and familiar *spirits,* forget my name, and lose my location, in the Name of Jesus.

I break all covenants of evil against my life. Python, Leviathan, all water *spirits*, I cancel all evil assignments against me, by the Fire in the Blood of Jesus.

All curses are broken by the power of the Holy Spirit and by the Blood of Jesus. Lord, give me resistance to resist all evil, so that I don't enter into evil covenants again, in the Name of Jesus.

I speak to you, Dream erasers, be set on Fire by the Holy Ghost.

Dream stealers, you are caught. We command you to stop stealing dreams and return all that was stolen back, in Jesus' Name.

Dream collectors, let go of my dreams, in the Name of Jesus.

Lord, let new and important dreams be given to me by the Holy Spirit of God.

Lord, let all my important dreams come back to me; and I call for new and vital dreams to come to me, in the Name of Jesus.

Lord, renew my health, wealth, and strengthen my family, and career, in Jesus' Name.

I pray for good successes, in the Name of Jesus, and by the power of the Holy Spirit.

All powers of darkness: anything in my bed, in my bedroom, in my house, that is from the pit of darkness, get out, get out, by Fire and by Force, in the Name of Jesus.

Holy Ghost Fire, burn all evil from my house, in the Name of Jesus.

Evil loads, receive Thunder Fire by the Holy Ghost, in the Name of Jesus.

I declare the Lord gives me divine rest, in the Name of Jesus.

I break all Evil covenants by the power in the Blood of Jesus, that I am not taken to any evil realms that are part of any satanic circles or satanic purposes in the night hours, in the Name of Jesus.

I declare that I receive power to remember my dreams. Lord, let me record my dreams and pray accordingly regarding what the Holy Spirit shows me from every dream, in the Name of Jesus.

Amen.

The Voids

If you are not living the abundant life that Jesus gave us, then there are voids in your life. Something or some *things* are missing or broken. There can be no void except for sin. We have all sinned, if you say you have not, then you lie. You cannot say that you have no voids, unless God has already perfected all matters that concern you and you live 100% in the Shalom of God.

Look at yourself, look at your life; are their voids, or have you reached the *form* of God? Take the log out of your eye and stop looking at the splinter in another person's. Most humans miss what's wrong with them for looking at others. This is why we must not war against flesh and blood we can see what's wrong with another person and not see our own faults or shortcomings.

Saints of God, warring against flesh and blood **is** walking after the flesh, in the most heinous, judgmental, and violent way. These are the things we are NOT supposed to do.

We declare war only if GOD says to declare war – else, it is sin; do not war against flesh and blood, no matter what you think or know someone has done to you. That includes little mini desperate housewives' wars, sibling, polygamous witchcraft, or evil associate's witchcraft. **Witchcraft is an expression of the nature of the devil.**

Sin causes man to take on the nature of the devil and rebel against the form that God created us for. This leads to voids and darkness in our souls. When we take on the nature of Christ, we begin to eradicate that formlessness and darkness. That's what we were put here to do outside of ourselves, but first we must get it out of ourselves.

> He that committeth sin is of the devil; for the devil sinneth from the beginning. For this purpose the Son of God was manifested, that he might destroy the works of the devil. (1 John 3:8)

Spend your time wisely, speaking over the face of the deep in your soul and your life, doing what it right, and transforming your *form* from glory to glory, from the inside, out.

Sin Keeps You Formless

Sin keeps you formless. You may even regress, and if you ever come out of that dark void, you may be far worse off than when you went in. Few plants thrive in the dark, but they still need some light. Sin shrouds the light in darkness. You won't be able to see physically, and you may not be able to discern, spiritually, what is bothering you in the dark. Even if it's a pesky demon *bizzing* around you like a mosquito and you're slapping at it but missing every time and only hitting and hurting yourself.

It'd be better to light that candle--, not just a citronella candle, but the spirit of man is the candle of the Lord. Build up your spirit man--, your candle of the Lord. Demons are relentless; therefore, you must be determined and diligent to grow your spirit man so you can arise in more power than they have.

Demons have no respect for your free will, no respect for your decision if you choose to do right, if you try to do right. And they also have no respect that you're saved. You would think that would make him leave you alone, no. *That* you're saved makes you more interesting to the Evil one.

Why?

Because before you were saved, you used to serve him; **you've defected**. The devil sees you as a runaway slave because you were not born saved; you were in sin before you accepted Christ.

You're especially attractive to the devil if you're a sinner, if you love sin, if you have ancestral iniquity in your bloodline, generational curses, demonic oppression by witchcraft, for example, that you may not even know anything about. It is best to sin not and to be prayed up; repent and seek deliverance down your family bloodline because you don't know what your folks have done or not done through the ages. None of us do.

So, Adam and Eve are in the garden. Here comes the devil with his advertising campaign. *Look at this tree. Look at this fruit. Ohh this will be good to eat.*

OK, but what did God say? Adam, did you tell Eve what God said? No. Eve went for the advertising campaign and shopped for the apple. I hate to say it, but women like to shop. So, the devil shows you the thing that he wants to lure you with. Satan knows that lust of the eyes, lust of the flesh, and pride of life help him to tempt people.

He may say, or the person may think, *Everyone else is doing it. Everybody else has it. Everybody else has done it. Nothing happened to them.*

Yes, it did. They died. They died spiritually. Do you have eyes to see that, or a Word of Knowledge to know it? Then read it in Genesis; they died.

This is where things get complicated. The devil would like folks to be dead, but if he can't have that, he'll take a piece of you.

What piece?

The piece that you're willing to sin with. The piece that you're willing to risk. Your hands, your ears, your mouth, some other body part. Your feet that are swift to run to sin. Because of unrepentant sin, your body parts may be compromised or diminished in the Spirit, and that will block your blessings. It could block your health. It could put you outside of the camp, at the gate. Whatever body part you decide you want to sin with is at risk and is also an access point to the ***apse*** of your heart.

Your soul, for instance, can be compromised or locked away. What does that even mean? I mean parts of your soul, such as your emotions, your feelings, or intellect could be compromised or locked away, spiritually speaking. By you not offering or not submitting your emotions, or any part of you to God for God to heal it, anything that you have on lockdown, it could already be stolen by the devil.

Blessings may no longer even be available to you because of sin and the choices you've made, the choice to have your emotions locked away. You know you don't love anybody; you can't love. You're not even trying. You don't forgive, you can't forgive.

In my ignorance, I used to hold on to unforgiveness. I was proud of it. That is not God's way. Unforgiveness is not just a state of mind or an emotion; it is an evil *spirit*--, a demon. There is no reason to hold on to it and let it embed itself into your soul. It will ruin your relationships and your life. Don't do it!

Or you could be stubborn in your will, and you can't stop being stubborn. You could be prideful. You have to be humble before the mighty hand of God, and with your family and your friends. Pride will get you nothing.

When you take God out of any part of your body, your soul, your spirit, your life, as before stated, those parts are instantly locked down. Now, it's open season for the devil against those parts that you have willingly, stubbornly locked down. Except the Lord watch, those that watch, watch in vain. Any part of your body that you lock down, because you don't want to be hurt like that again, you don't want to hurt anymore, or for any self-justified reason, is a big mistake. YOU do not have the ability to guard it and keep the devil away from it. Only when God is in your heart, soul, life and **even your money** will it be guarded. Mark my words.

All of your choices are not just about you. When curses are allowed into a life, if they don't get you, and sometimes even if they do, they are now lined up to get your children and your *children's* children. You have now polluted the bloodline of your family.

The devil and witches most often work ***outside of time.*** For this reason, unless you break a curse and call expiration on it, it doesn't expire in your bloodline.

Choose ye this day. It's a binary choice. It's A or B. It's light or dark. It's good or bad. It's one or the other. It's not a little good, and a little bad, it's one or the other. But because of the curse that you caused to come upon you, because it doesn't happen right away, Yeah, it could be days--, but more often, it's months, weeks, years before that curse actually shows up in your life. And then all of a sudden you have no idea what caused the curse, no idea, and no ownership of what caused the curse in your life, because man has a tendency to forget. But you didn't just *cause* the curse in **your** life. You've caused it all the way down your family line for generations, at least to the third of the fourth, maybe even to the 10th generation if God perceives you or the next generation, or the next in your family line hates Him.

- Lord, I repent of every sin I have ever sinned against You; please have Mercy on me and forgive me, in the Name of Jesus.
- Lord, I repent for the sins of my parents and the sins of my ancestors going all the way back to Adam and Eve, in the Name of Jesus.
- I break every curse in my life, by the power in the Blood of Jesus.
- I break the evil covenant that allows the curse. I bind every demon sent to enforce the curse. I dismantle the bondage and the evil yokes put upon me because of this curse.
- Whom the Son sets free is free indeed. Lord, set me free today, in the Name of Jesus.
  Amen.

Jesus Finished the *Work*

Jesus, the Son of Man, who was already the son of God, **in flesh** *became* a Son of God. That is how He finished His soul work. Jesus did that, and it was announced when John the Baptist baptized Jesus and that dove alighted on Jesus. It was not until after that that Jesus began His Earthly ministry.

Jesus finished the soul work to reach the completed, perfected form of the image of God proving that it could be done.

So, what are we doing?

We too, must stop being formless or not fully formed, and become a son of God and then proceed with purpose toward destiny.

One must make one's flesh comply with SONSHIP. The spirit is willing, but the flesh is weak. The flesh tests the spirit by earthly temptations, tests, and trials. **Unless you pay attention to your dreams, these tests and trials are unannounced.**

Under stressful conditions will you behave just like everyone else? Or, will you be different? Under certain flesh conditions will you behave like your unsaved neighbor, or is the Spirit of God in you to a measure that makes you different? Godly? That is not just the question, that is the test. Often. Daily.

Age of Accountability

There came a time in your life where you reached the age of accountability. In some cultures, they commemorate that as a coming of age. There are rites of passage, and celebrations, and that is when you receive new responsibilities, respect, and authority.

That happens in the spirit, too. Everyone must grow up, if you resist, it will be forced upon you. Even in that forcing, you still have free will and you can reject discipline, growth, forming and *becoming*. That is ill-advised because you will get nowhere in life without discipline and maturity. Kids who are born in homes with little to no discipline do anything they want, eat anything they want and disobey everyone that they want. But in this life, they will be disciplined. They will be disciplined somewhere, somehow. By teachers in school? Possibly. By joining the

Military? Definitely. By the police force because they are frequent law breakers? Possibly, but this is perilous because the police in a lot of countries have become so unpredictable and dangerous. Folks, it's best to color within the lines, and stay out of trouble. Get your discipline from loving parents and from God before you go out into those streets.

Discipline and diligence are integral in your becoming a son of God and leaving formlessness behind.

Slimed

Slimed is how I describe being defiled. The sons of God (Genesis 6:6) could not go into God's creation as God had created it so they had to defile it first – slime it, then it was corrupted and unprotected because of sin. Now that person can be attacked by the agents of darkness.

On legal grounds that is called entrapment, but spiritually, the devil does it all the time. Man gets in trouble for the sin that the devil caused or even enticed that man to commit.

The devil is a legalist; he has no Mercy and no Grace. What, you think he has the Fruit of the Spirit? He doesn't have that Spirit so there is no way he will have the fruit of it. Any display of such is FAKE; it is an act and a masquerade.

Satan will use the tiniest little sin that he can get you to commit to gain access to mess you up. Like the Earth, you are made of clay, you are made of *earth*, and like the Earth, sin messes you up. When darkness covers a man, that takes away order and leaves voids, it blocks Light and sponsors more darkness.

God is not the author of confusion, whereas the devil loves confusion; it is where he hides and operates, and then hides again.

Sin is the cause of a man getting *slimed* and defiled.

God hates slime. In Bible days, when one was slimed, *that is*, defiled, that person sat at the gate outside of the city for a day, a whole day--, until a new batch of tender mercies that were new every morning was granted to us by God.

Do you realize that outside the gate means that your worship that day will not reach the Throne Room of God? Your sacrifice won't be received, and your prayers won't be heard. On the day of sinning, sliming, or defiling you cannot come into the presence of God--, for a whole day.

Better is one day in the Courts of the Lord; the psalmist must have known something about that.

> For a day in thy courts is better than a thousand. I had rather be a doorkeeper in the house of my God, than to dwell in the tents of wickedness.
> (Psalm 84:10)

You wanted to sin? Well, it's like the kid who wants to be disobedient who has to go to their room to think about what they've done. At the gate, outside the city we are stuck in "our room," away from the rest of the family, and away from the family activities, to think about what we've done, and prayerfully **repent**. When you sin, you are choosing to be outside of, not in the will of God, or in the presence of God--, or the family --, the Body of Christ.

Jewish law was such that if that is what you want, then have at it, but you'd be on your own after that.

Jews offered morning sacrifices, afternoon offerings, evening offerings, peace offerings, sin offerings, and so forth. Outside of the gate for one whole day means you didn't just miss a 1-minute TikTok "Bible quote" Bible study, you missed the presence of God for an entire day.

Being outside of the presence of your husband, wife, boyfriend, or girlfriend is heart wrenching to the average person who is really in love. If you don't miss God when you are outside the *gates*, how is your love life with God?

If you couldn't call your spouse because you're outside the coverage area, you might freak out. If you're outside the Gate, you are outside of the coverage area to *call on* God.

The picture that counters all this void, the picture of what the puzzle is supposed to look like is in the Word of God, it shows the image of what you're supposed to look like when you put on Christ.

While you were stuck outside the Gate, God, had made Himself available that day to work on, or continue to work on your FORM, to re-member you, to put you back together the way He designed you to be. You change from glory to glory and strength to strength in His presence, and that takes time. But that day, in the day of sin or defilement, you do not work on your voids because we need God to repair the breaches created by sin. Work stops for a day when you have no access to God's presence that day.

The only good news about that is that in Jewish custom a day is *any part* of that day, so **REPENT** to shorten your punishment time and again seek the presence of God.

The person who stopped your work is also working to unravel the progress that you've made in your life so far.

DO NOT COME DOWN FROM THAT WALL. Don't let those with the spirits of Sanballat and Tobias taunt you and make you come down from repairing the voids in your walls, in your soul, in your life. The enemy is trying to stop the work of the building of the Temple. You, also are the temple of the Holy Spirit.

> What? know ye not that your body is the temple of the Holy Ghost which is in you, which ye have of God, and ye are not your own?
> (1 Corinthians 6:19)

If you were building a house and the contractors did not show up for a whole day, you'd probably be upset. Well, God is building you ---, God shows up, but **where are you**? At Johnny's house? Doing what? Sinning? Or, hiding because of sin? Or hiding so you can sin? Are you *outside* the gate? Where are you?

Where are you, Y*our Voidness?* No, not your royal highness, as you are supposed to be a king and should be addressed with dignity. But since you are still without *form*, building and then tearing down over and again, by sinning, you are creating voids instead of working toward the high calling and toward finishing the work--, therefore, *Your Voidness--*, where are you?

As long as you are *without form,* and not in the form, image, and likeness of God, you can only be addressed as *Your Voidness. Sorry.*

But there is hope. As long as we have life, we have hope. (Ecclesiastes 9:4).

Without the Holy Spirit and one-another ministry, we may not recognize that we have voids, or know if we have wrong things within our voids. Evil *spirits* (demons) occupy the dark voids in our souls. This is why we should endeavor not to have any voids because they will be filled by the enemy. We have to unseat those evil *spirits* from our souls.

There is hope by the Grace and Mercy of God.

- Every power of the gate and every power of wicked elders to make me what God did not create me to be, DIE, in the Name of Jesus.
- Power of evil gates, power of wicked elders that is sponsoring the enterprise of sin in my life, backfire, in the Name of Jesus.
- Every dark and evil *spirit*, in my soul trying to make me take on their nature, die out of my soul, in the Name of Jesus.
- Every dark and evil *spirit*, leading me to sin, die out of my soul, in the Name of Jesus.

Amen.

Entropy: War in Heaven

Mom and dad bring home a new baby. The older one or ones who are already there may have mixed emotions about their new sibling.

Satan was designed and built to worship God, but he rebelled, and a war broke out in Heaven. Take note that if you plan to rebel against God, and do so repeatedly and without repentance, Satan, who fell from Heaven, like lightning, cannot protect you from the judgement of God, even though the devil may have been the one who enticed you to sin. Case in point: Satan fell, like lightning from Heaven for his pride and rebellion.

God is now seeking those who will worship Him in Spirit and in Truth; God is seeking worshippers. God is seeking real worshippers. The devil wouldn't worship, so man was created in God's own image and likeness--, <u>to worship God.</u>

Man was created for worship, and he is a worship machine. He will worship something or someone all day, all night if possible. This is why the devil wants the soul of man so that he can steal man's worship for himself, thereby empowering himself with that worship, and keeping man from worshipping God.

He who worships God, God will glorify. As long as a man is not worshipping God, he will be lackluster and not glorified; he will be void and *without form* in one or more aspects of his life and being. Man was created by God and crowned with glory and honor—glory is part of the program; it is part of the *form*. Until you are glorified by God, you have not reached your destiny *form*.

Worship can be stolen and milked out of man in many ways. What you look at, give attention to, follow, spend time with, celebrate, enjoy, and repeatedly do is all worship.

When God put Adam and Eve in the Garden at Eden, their job was to minister to the

Garden--, their work, their assigned purpose **is** worship. Do you have a Godly job, or an ungodly, unwholesome job? Whatever you are doing from 9 to 5 is a form of worship; I pray it honors God and serves mankind.

Not Falling Apart

Of all the things you could have declared, decreed, or spoken into existence, prophetically, let it not be that you are falling apart. Saints of God, we don't talk like that. We were already born in sin and shaped in iniquity, we've got to come back from that, and part of how that is done is with the words of our mouth, with our own breath, just like God. We do not use our own words to destroy ourselves, or our future. Sometimes what we think we are saying right now is only for today, but you are speaking into the future--, your future, your spouse's, family's and the future of your loved and *hated* ones.

So many people are complaining that they are "falling apart" when they are here to create *form* and substance out of void and darkness that they may have been born into, or sinned and gotten themselves into. They should be speaking and prophesying over their own lives and the futures of their children.

God's Word will not return to Him void; so, shall it be. Therefore, you have that same authority – to speak into your own life and future instead of *grasshoppering* around doing nothing in your youth when life was good or easy and you took everything for granted.

If you wait until something happens then you will need a mighty power and deliverance, to get out of trouble. Instead of waiting, you can regularly speak so that NOTHING ungodly happens to you. I am serious: A man can have whatever he says.

Over the counter supplements and cures, for example, like good food are more for maintenance, **keeping** you healthy rather than quickly reversing disease. If they reverse disease it takes huge doses or a long time. Most often you should not use a large dose of an *over-the-counter* supplement, as it may be toxic, but even if it is not, if you are really sick, you may not have time for it to work to cure or heal you.

Even though the leaves on the trees are for the healing of the nations, we are supposed to be in divine health. The way that is done could be what we are not doing. Yes, diet, exercise – but there are some predilections that run in families. So, in spiritual mapping, one must find out what runs in their family and deal with it head on--, immediately, and regularly. We don't just pray once about a thing. Yes, we believe God heard and that He answered, so we thank, praise, and worship Him for hearing and answering, even if the answer hasn't manifested yet. That is called faith.

If your dad has high blood pressure, you don't just feel sorry for your dad or believe that because you're 22 it won't happen to you. Don't expect it to happen to you; don't get faith for it. Instead, start praying against that disease as soon as you see it, for your family member, and speak that it will not continue to you or into your generations. Sickness, and diseases such as HBP is a curse, and all diseases have spiritual origins. So, waiting until it happens and then beginning generic prayers, or taking over the counter meds for it is far less effective than praying prophetically about the issues that run in your family, in your bloodline.

Saints of God, we don't accept curses just because there is medication available for it; it is still a curse. Jesus received 39 stripes for our healing so that the diseases of the Egyptians would not be put upon us. If you, yourself had received 39 lashes across your back so that no disease should come upon you and you woke up with a runny nose one morning, wouldn't you be quick to speak against that threatening cold? Wouldn't you remember that whip across your back? So, if we don't use what Jesus has done and appropriated for us, then are we not appreciative? Did He receive those stripes for nothing?

What is the cause of that particular curse that runs in your family? Whatever it is, that disease is expressed now in the DNA of your family, but it started out as a singular curse. Was it from unrepented sin? Was it sent by a witch or wizard and never resisted by the first victim in your family? It's in the blood of the family now.

Most likely, the curse of the Law is not only a curse, it is full of additional curses. Curses really slime a person and *slimed* means that more curses can alight.

At any age, but especially as a young person of accountable age, you should be speaking into your own future. How many kids have answered the what to you want to be when you grow up question? Probably all. Teach your kids what they want to be, not vocationally, necessarily, but spiritually, physically and in their soul. They want to be healthy, wealthy, and wise, yes. And they want prospered souls. They want to be all that God has planned for them to be. They want to be successful in life and in good health. They want to be emotionally and mentally balanced, even peaceful. They want to finish schooling with a good education at the right age. They want to marry the right spouse at the right time in their life. They want to have the right number of healthy children at the times appointed by God. They want to serve God and avoid devil traps. They want to do the will of God, live long and prosper, in the Name of Jesus.

And, you want those same things for yourself, don't you? You may think of more. Don't just pray those things in secret for your child. Speak those things over your child, often. Pray with your child when they reach the age of understanding.

The things you want for yourself include long life and good health, I'm sure. Pray for that and speak those things over yourself and your spouse. Make sure your spouse is praying and prophesying the Word of God over you, as well.

Do you think when men lived for 100's of years that they suffered in "old age"? Methuselah lived to be 965 years old, do you think he had the diseases that we consider to be diseases of old age for 900 years and still lived? With no meds? Do you think that God just touched him every so often to magically keep diseases off of him? (Yes, every morning tender mercies.)

Or, do you think that Methusaleh's mouth was agreeing with divine health, starting at an early age?

If you spent a lifetime obsessed with your own body, worshipping it, or suffering and trying to heal it, the devil would be pleased about that. A sick body is not the form that God intended for us. We should be whole in our body, soul and spirit; that is the will of God for us who are in Christ Jesus. Amen.

Dismantled

Saints of God, you are not falling apart. You're in the Earth so if something physical or other is not working, that means that the prince of this world has already either dismantled you, or because of your sin, or the sins of your ancestors, the devil may be in the *process* of dismantling you. You may not know when he started, but it's reached a critical point now and you can feel it; something hurts.

God builds, the devil destroys. God adds a block, the devil knocks it off–, if the devil has access. You're the one who either blocks the devil or gives him access. You. It is you by your own choices, daily. And by the sins of your ancestors, that you may choose to repent on their behalf for them, or let that iniquity stand and attack your life. You decide.

What God made, designed, built and breathed life into does not just FALL apart. It must be dismantled. If the devil is dismantling anything God made or anything God put in place, he's had to bypass a lot of protections that God put in place, that the victim has ignored.

There is no comparing God-made and manmade.

Because of sin in the Earth and iniquity down your family line, disassembling may have begun before you were ever born. That means everyone born in this family has this problem or that problem, but the same problem. It's in the DNA now, so it is inherited.

What do I mean?

Some families have genetic issues or medical conditions, the devil already began in your bloodline, and you simply inherited the family issue. Those problems could be spiritual, soulish, or physical or any combination of those three, since we are triune beings.

As a simple example, your mom and / or your dad had crowded teeth and had to wear braces. Your baby teeth look really cute and don't even have spaces between them like other kids. Your parents may have bragged on how straight and even your baby teeth were.

Well folks, that's bad. There should be spaces. Anyhoo, here come the adult teeth, crowded in the mouth and crooked with a vengeance. Crowded teeth are not only expensive to treat, many times there is pain and discomfort and many procedures may have to be done in that mouth. That's bad enough, but then the devil is causing you to have to spend money that others with well aligned teeth don't have to spend.

No, you don't become angry with your parents; they didn't know. They probably just hoped your teeth would be okay. Don't blame the dentist, the workman is worthy of pay. This was a spiritual issue not addressed way, way, down the line in the past of your family. It is what it is right now. Pray that the devil can't get anywhere else into your life, body, or finances. And, sin not.

The devil wants to break you down for parts.

What parts?

Mostly he wants your soul. The soul has parts. Divide and conquer is still his strategy.

It's bad. Don't be a hooptey up on blocks letting the devil continue to dismantle you, your future, and your bloodline.

Don't Come Down off the Wall

No matter what you think you're doing, you're building something. People think they are building a career, education, family, a house, a ministry --, and yes you are. But first and foremost, you are building **yourself**. As said, Jesus had to become a Son of God before His ministry really started. Could this be why we see so many broken and failed pastors in pulpits, they weren't fully *formed* before they climbed to the platform? Or, perhaps God didn't call them, so they took the stage and not the pulpit?

God knows.

The void form that you were conceived in sin and shaped in iniquity needs <u>**work**</u>. Yes, thank God if you were born to term and according to doctors you were whole and perfect as a newborn.

Folks, no matter what the doctors made your parents believe, and then your parents made you believe, you were not born perfect, you are not perfect and unless you have God on board you are not getting more perfect each day. Quite the opposite, really. No one is born spiritually perfect, but doctors and nurses and parents don't look at that aspect of a newborn; their concern is physical and medical. In addition, we all are born with immature, unprospered souls that need to be ministered to and *formed*.

Forty weeks in your mother's womb is a great start—, physically. Everything you need to grow to a full sized, functioning human adult, in the natural world is in the DNA code that you inherit from your parents.

What you need to become a proper functioning Christian human being is in the code of God. It is in the Word, in the Spirit and found in every Word that proceeds out of God's mouth for your life. What you need to **first** become a son of God is in the Spirit, in the Word and in the *proceeding* Word of God for your life.

Before that, however, what do you have to *undo*? Someone said that the most successful people will be those who can unlearn what is incorrect and then learn what is correct. We all must unlearn lies and learn Truth. We have to apply Truth and grow and develop and *become*.

Your destiny is too big, and it is too important for you not to do this work, while you have life, for the night comes when no man can work.

In this building you are also building or adding on to the foundation of your family's bloodline. Sometimes you may have to go back to go forward. Some may have to take down faulty ancestral foundations and ask the Lord to rebuild it to proper specifications.

No matter how you build your life, it will impact your children and your children's children. Don't wait until your children get here to decide that you want to start doing things right; start now so you will be prepared, and your children and generations won't have to suffer as you may have. Start as soon as you reach that age of accountability speaking and working to build a Godly life that will sustain and bless your generations.

You Are A Prophet

A man can have what he says. When you get enough discernment to see what you need and then say it in the affirmative, in the positive, prophesying it, you will change, and your situations will change.

It is this writer's opinion that old age and senior moments are the results of **not prophesying Godly words over your own life**. I believe aging in general is from not speaking the Godly Word over yourself, your life, your health, body, career, success, regularly and often, even from when you first reached accountability. If you speak no Word, you will get a result, but it will be the *default* of Earth. The devil is the prince of this world; he is running this, until you invite God into it and run the devil out of it you will only get what the devil wants for you.

If you speak negative words over yourself, you will hasten the dismantling of even what God has given you from the womb, coupled with what your ancestors have left you, good or bad.

People form ideas about education, what school they want to go to. Ideas are pondered over about who and when to marry. More words are spoken regarding having children, a house, car, et cetera. Who speaks into their future of their life and health? Parents, that's your job until the child comes of age, then the child agrees with the parents; there is much more power in numbers, especially in prayer and in speaking and prophesying.

But, no, most just sit back and "watch it happen", expecting the same results their parents got, or the same results that others get. Or, worse, expecting different results when nothing has changed, or things have changed for the worse. People, please. Please. Please pray and say what God says about you and over your life and situations.

Just because those around you are getting sick after a certain age doesn't mean you have to--, especially if you have done the work to

not get sick. Oh, we think that's eating vegetables and cardboard and having no fun at all. I, personally think it is fun to NOT be sick. If we've done the work in our youth to be rid of yokes that will brace, grip and hurt us in our maturity, then we should have good results and good health, unless there are time-stamped bloodline ambushes waiting for the golden years. If we've done nothing, we may get what the "doctors" say. If we have only done what everyone else has done, we will get those same results. Period.

Reject that *que sera sera* attitude, that what will be will be, it is what it is. Reject all of those things are what the devil says will be. If you want something different, you have to **be** different, talk differently, have faith for **different**. That different should be of God and God's way; all else is just laying down and letting life run all over you.

Of course, there is the drama of sudden destruction, sudden illness and the rushing to doctors and hospitals for the emergency cure or fix. Thank God for medicines and Godly physicians, but what did you do leading up to this? Did you just take the good days as long as you could, waiting for and dreading the day things might turn stormy or get bad for you? That, my friend, if you profess Christianity, is a *form* of godliness, denying the power thereof. If you don't use the power that God gives you, then it is power that is denied.

God is the Ancient of Days, and we don't hear about God ever being sick, and He's old. Of course, God is all Spirit, and Spirits don't have flesh that will corrupt or rot – or age.

Your spirit man will KEEP your flesh; have you spoken to your spirit man? What is your spirit man doing? Have you given your spirit man anything to do?

Have you spoken to the voids in your life? Have you spoken to what may be squatting in the voids in your life? Or will you let what will be, just *be*? Have you spoken to your form and told it to put on Christ and adhere to His image and likeness, for which you were created?

Your thoughts have created your words, and your words have created your reality – even your future.

Kingdom Spouse, *Anyone*?

Do you know how many times you've said disparaging things about your dating and marriage situation? You must renounce and undo all of that because all of that only spoke to the Void of your dating life, the formlessness of your romantic and married life.

The term, *kingdom spouse* is not in the Bible; however, I enjoy using it because it differentiates a soul from being any random whosoever versus a saved, set aside single of God who is available and seeking a Godly marriage. It differentiates a marital partner from a *spirit spouse*--, which is a demon that will marry you with every plan to take up permanent residence in your soul--, in the voids in your soul. The term, Kingdom spouse separates it from being any of the named things that the world and witches call a *spouse* such as a twin flame, which is not even a real thing.

God does not split souls; tell me where is that in the Bible?

Exactly.

So, there is no such thing as a *twin soul*. Don't talk that witchcraft talk, else you may summon a demon.

Also, God doesn't like it when souls are tied because that makes a mockery of God's matrimonial covenant. Soul ties include the devil in an ungodly three-fold cord.

Where Are Your Children?

Are you one who is looking for the fruit of the womb; are you looking to conceive and have children? I know of many who have tried for years and years and finally succeeded at having their own children. I know of others who did not succeed.

Many are the children of the world. Our God, however, is looking for righteous seed. No, I'm not saying anything is wrong with your kids. As said before God wants more than one son and that starts in folks with Godly seed.

Man's DNA can reproduce the physical, but when it comes to the spiritual—that is where there may be a loss of *form*. Many are the children of unrighteousness, but where are the righteous?

As a whole, are people getting more sick, or healthier? Darwin's theory of survival of the fittest makes me ask are we multiplying to *more* fitness, better looking, stronger, smarter? Or, did we forget God? Did we forget the *image* of God? Is that why we are looking void and more formless? **When we look more like God, so will our *seed*.**

Jacob put out stakes to cause his cattle to multiply after the *kind* they saw, which were spotted, speckled, and streaked. If we are looking at Jesus, we should reproduce after *that kind* because we will **become** *that kind*. Saints of the Lord: BEHOLD YOUR GOD.

When you Behold your God, you will reproduce smarter, brighter, healthier, and more spiritual offspring. What have you produced so far? Do you have happy, successful children? Have you spoken the Word of God over your children? Have you prophesied over them, or has fear sponsored the words spoken in your home throughout the years and decades?

If you speak what you don't want, you are still prophesying. That's very dangerous because someone or some ***thing*** is always listening. Depending on the spiritual makeup of your home and environment, a *spirit* will take those words and run as far as they can to create that situation that you spoke in your life. Speak good words, only; speak God words.

You are a prophet over your own life and over your children's lives, so guard your words. But speak those words. In your proper form you will look and behave as God. In the beginning God created he Heaven and the Earth --, by speaking.

Life is in the blood and the blood that you carry is also given to your children. What is in that blood must and shall be expressed at some point – at some time – sooner, or later.

Surely, you've noticed how it is nearly impossible to get blood off of or out of anything. Blood and DNA is what gets criminals caught. It is the blood. Because of that, what is in the blood is also there for expression, unless the Blood of Jesus overrides it. God can take us out of our polluted blood.

It's So Easy

You have this authority, and what you're praying to God about, what you want God to do for you is easy for God. But it could be that God is waiting for you to do it, since He has imparted His Spirit to you.

Therefore, you are well able to do it yourself. Just breathe. And when you breathe, make sure you're speaking the Word of God. And you too can make easy work of these *nations,* the evil darkness that tries to encroach upon your life, steal your blessings, and take the goodness and the sweetness out of your life. You can get rid of those spiritual frat boys who want to live it up, party and make you take on their nature.

Call for the consuming Fire of God to consume the evil nations that rise up against you. Those nations will be defeated and depart from you, by your breath.

So, breathe.

You will give praise and worship to God by doing that, and that's what you were put here to do. And you'll become a son of God. Isn't that your goal, to finish the work and reach your desired FORM?

When you are breathing, and speaking and praying and declaring and conquering, that is how sons of God behave. When you finally reach this place The Spirit can say to the Father, **Behold Your son.**

And, son, behold your Father--, behold Your Father, God.

Jesus, behold your brother. Of course they will already know you by the Spirit, but what a glorious introduction that will be.

Further, the realms of darkness, the evil nations, spiritual wickedness, and the like will know who you are as well. They may already know because you will be known in spiritual realms. Not one of them will mock you with, *Jesus, I know, Paul, I know, but who are you?*

Where Is God's Son?

Are you *forming*? Are you in process? Are you *becoming*? Is this steady work? Or, is it stop and go?

Any man who has put his hand to the plow should not turn back. Humans sometimes fall, but we must get back up. Sometimes we relapse, sometimes we are tricked, ambushed, or sabotaged. Get back up and get back to serving the Lord.

Paul says that we are predestined to be conformed to the image of God's Son, (Romans 8:18-30). We are to be conformed to the image of His Son, that is Jesus Christ. And that Christ is the first begotten of many brothers.

Those beholding the Lord's glory are being transformed into the same image from one degree of glory to another. What you look at, what you behold, you will emulate, unconsciously, and then you will ultimately reproduce after that *kind*.

The desired image, of course, is the image of God, (2 Corinthians 3:18). The divine Son of God, Jesus is our Supermodel, and we should be changing, conforming, and transforming into the image of Christ. Jesus was 100% man and 100% God. We, who are in the flesh have that 100%-man part down, now we put on Christ to change from being *spiritually* formless, in disarray, unsettled, unstable, or like the devil to becoming more and more like God, by following after Christ.

We put on the new man, and we are renewed by the renewing of our minds. We renew the mind by revelation and knowledge; both are power, and they brings deliverance, change, transformation, and **stability**.

We were created in the image and likeness of God. Man fell. Jesus came to Earth to redeem us. It is now up to us to put on Christ and become more like Jesus every day so we can be fully restored back into relationship with God. In that, we are given the opportunity to become sons of God and that means we work on that every day until we reach Godly perfection, which is only possible in Christ.

When you achieve the form of godliness that does not deny the power therof, then you become a son of God. All your voids and amorphousness is gone. God is well-pleased and then you may be enrobed in the glory that is due man and imbued with certain power from God. You'll no longer be without form, but even though you may have suffered the burning desolation when you were in sin and afar off from God, you will now have been redeemed, restored, and like Christ, you will have finished your work. You can be among the few men that are left. You will be called a son of God.

> Therefore hath the curse **devoured** the earth, and they that dwell therein are desolate: therefore the inhabitants of the earth are burned, and few men left. Isaiah 24:6

When you achieve **form**, when you attain to your correct form, you know what you believe in and you can give anyone the reasons why you believe in God. You, as iron may have been sharpened by iron; that is not always painless, but it is necessary. You are now deep and can call on Deep, and when Deep answers you, you will have *understanding*. You may have been malleable and therefore that iron was able to sharpen you, bringing you to your correct form.

Thank God that you are no longer mutable, you are not unstable, you are a solid son of God. You are not unstable like water, like Reuben. You are not unstable like a disembodied *spirit*. You are spirit. You have a soul, you live in a body, and you firmly know who you are, in Christ.

You are secure in who you are and in Him you move, breathe, and have your being. We, like Christ, desire that not one be lost, but if many do not find their way or sadly, reject the Lord, then Lord, let us be among the few who find it.

- Lord, empower us to be a help to those who are having difficulty finding their way, in the Name of Jesus.

- Lord, have Mercy on us all and give us more Grace and time as You guide us with and into Your marvelous Light.
- Thank You, Lord for allowing us to reach stability and our **form** which is also expressed in *agape* Love for one another.
- Lord, because we are like You, we can Love, but we also war when it is necessary. In our divine nature which we have put on, we can do whatever is needful, in the Name of Jesus.

AMEN.

Psalm 18:37-50

I have pursued my enemies and
overtaken them;
Neither did I turn back again till they
were destroyed.

I have wounded them,
So that they could not rise;
They have fallen under my feet.
For You have armed me with
strength for the battle;

You have subdued under me those
who rose up against me.

You have also given me the necks of
my enemies,
So that I destroyed those who hated
me.
They cried out, but *there was* none to
save;
Even to the LORD, but He did not
answer them.

Then I beat them as fine as the dust

before the wind;
I cast them out like dirt in the streets.

You have delivered me from the
strivings of the people;
You have made me the head of
the nations;

A people I have not known shall
serve me.

As soon as they hear of me they obey
me;
The foreigners submit to me.

The foreigners fade away,
And come frightened from their
hideouts.

The LORD lives!
Blessed *be* my Rock!

Let the God of my salvation be
exalted.

It is God who avenges me,
And subdues the peoples under me;

He delivers me from my enemies.
You also lift me up above those who
rise against me;

You have delivered me from the
violent man.

Therefore I will give thanks to You,
O LORD, among the Gentiles,
And sing praises to Your name.

Great deliverance He gives to His
king,
And shows mercy to His anointed,
To David and his descendants
forevermore.

Amen.

Dear Reader

Thank you for acquiring and reading this book. I pray that it impacts your *form* and your desire to become a son of the Only Living God.

May you glorify Jehovah in your living.

In your patience possess ye your souls. May your whole soul be preserved blameless, in the Name of Jesus.

God of peace sanctify you through and through, in Jesus' Name.

I bless you, in the Name of Jesus.

Amen.

Dr. Marlene Miles

Other books by this author
(related or mentioned titles are pictured with links)

AK: The Adventures of the Agape Kid

AMONG SOME THIEVES

Ancestral Powers

Blindsided: *Has the Old Man Bewitched You?*

https://a.co/d/5O2fLLR

Churchzilla, The Wanna-Be, Supposed-to-be Bride of Christ

Darkness

Demons Hate Questions

Devil Weapons: Unforgiveness, Bitterness,...

Dream Defilement https://a.co/d/4f4P3Et

Don't Refuse Me, Lord (4 book series)

Every Evil Bird

Evil Touch

Failed Assignment

Fantasy Spirit Spouse

FAT Demons (The): *Breaking Demonic Curses*

The Fold (4 book series)
- The Fold (Book 1)
- Name Your Seed (Book 2)
- The Poor Attitudes of Money (3)
- Do Not Orphan Your Seed

got HEALING? Verses for Life

got LOVE? Verses for Life

got HOPE? Verses for Life

got money?

How to Dental Assist

How to Dental Assit2: Be Productive, Not Wasteful

Let Me Have A Dollar's Worth

Living for the NOW of God
https://a.co/d/1pwGkJJ

Lose My Location https://a.co/d/crD6mV9

Man Safari, *The (mini book)*

Marriage Ed. Rules of Engagement & Marriage Made Perfect in Love

Motherboard (The) - soul prosperity series

Plantation Souls

Power Money: Nine Times the Tithe

The Power of Wealth *(forthcoming)*

Seasons of Grief

Seasons of War

Sift You Like Wheat

Soul Prosperity soul prosperity series 3

https://a.co/d/5p8YvCN

Souls Captivity soul prosperity series 2

The Spirit of Poverty

This Is NOT That: How to Keep Demons from Coming At You

Throne of Grace: Courtroom Prayer

Time Is of the Essence   https://a.co/d/1w4V5o9

Too Many Wives: *Why You Have Lady Problems*

Tormenting Spirits https://a.co/d/dAogEJf

Triangular Power *(series)*

- Powers Above
- SUNBLOCK
- Do Not Swear by the Moon
- STARSTRUCK

Uncontested Doom

Upgrade: How to Get Out of Survival Mode

- **Toxic Souls** (Book 2 of series)
- **Legacy** (Book 3 of series)

Warfare Prayer Against Beauty Curses

Warfare Prayer Against Poverty

What Have You to Declare?

When the Devourer is Rebuked (mini book)

When You See Blood https://a.co/d/apvdjvW

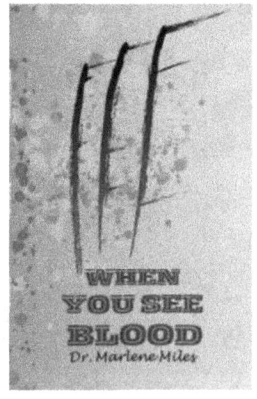

The Wilderness Romance *(series)*

- *The Social Wilderness*
- *The Sexual Wilderness*
- *The Spiritual Wilderness*

Without Form

Series

The Fold (a series on Godly finances)
https://a.co/d/4hz3unj

Soul Prosperity Series https://a.co/d/bz2M42q

Spirit Spouse books

https://a.co/d/9VehDSo

https://a.co/d/97sKOwm

Thieves of Darkness series

Triangular Powers https://a.co/d/aUCjAWC

Upgrade (series) *How to Get Out of Survival Mode*
https://a.co/d/aTERhXO

Notes:

www.ingramcontent.com/pod-product-compliance
Lightning Source LLC
Chambersburg PA
CBHW060841050426
42453CB00008B/780